I0135898

Odie Explores
A Paw Smart Book

By: D.S. Provance

Odie Explores
Paw Smart Series #2

Text and Photographs by D.S. Provance
Original Paw Smart Design by A.J. Stawarz

All rights reserved. No part of this publication may be
reproduced, stored in a retrieval system or transmitted
in any form or by any means without the prior written
permission of the author, except by a reviewer who may
quote brief passages as part of a review.

© 2018, D.S. Provance
Crimson Gold Publishing

Remember, like people, dogs and other animals are unique
individuals with their own personalities.

Contact information:
inquiries@dsprovance.com
www.dsprovance.com

ISBN: 978-0-9986309-1-5

To David

Exploring
is fun!
Let's go.

Hi. My name is Odin, but my friends call me Odie.

I am an explorer. You are too if you like finding and learning new things.

I am teaching Phoebe how to explore. She is my new friend and neighbor. Join us as we discover what is in our neighborhood.

Walking is a great way to explore outside.

As we walk, our eyes look for things that move and our ears listen for new sounds. Our noses find smelly things.

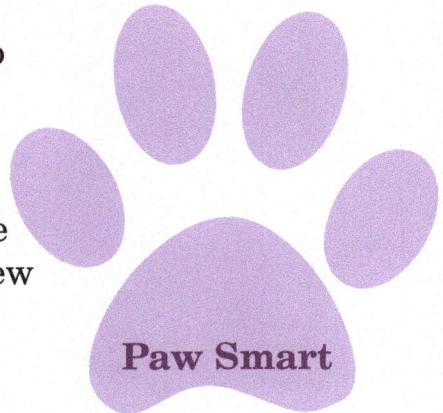

Paw Smart

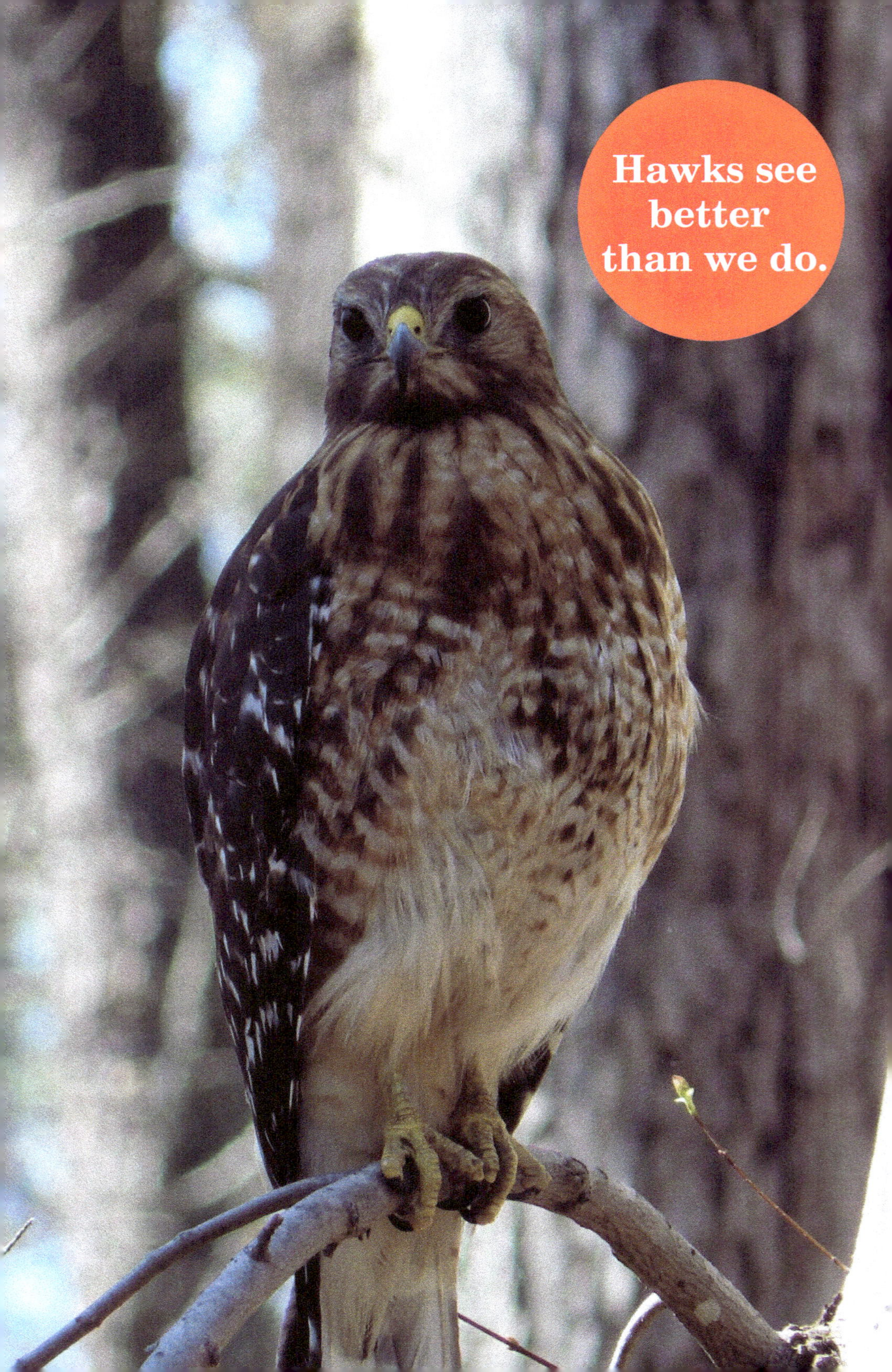

Hawks see better than we do.

Look, a red-shouldered hawk is sitting on that tree.

I saw it turn its head to watch us. Hawks are hunters, but we're too big to eat.

Hawks can see a tiny mouse while flying above the trees. Hawks eat mice, snakes, squirrels, and other small animals.

When red-shouldered hawks call to each other, they are very loud.

Hawks cannot whisper, and they do not sing like songbirds. Hawks are very quiet when they hunt.

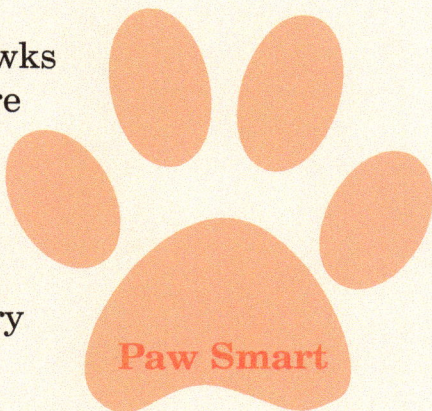

Paw Smart

Wrens eat tiny garden pests.

Listen to those singing songbirds.

My favorites are little brown Carolina wrens. Every spring, I find speckled eggs inside my flower pots.

Wren chicks are pink and fuzzy. They don't open their eyes for several days. Two weeks after hatching, they look like their parents and fly away.

Chicks are baby birds. Some chicks have special names.

An eyas is a baby hawk. A duckling is a baby duck. A poult is a baby chicken or turkey.

Paw Smart

Oak trees grow from acorns.

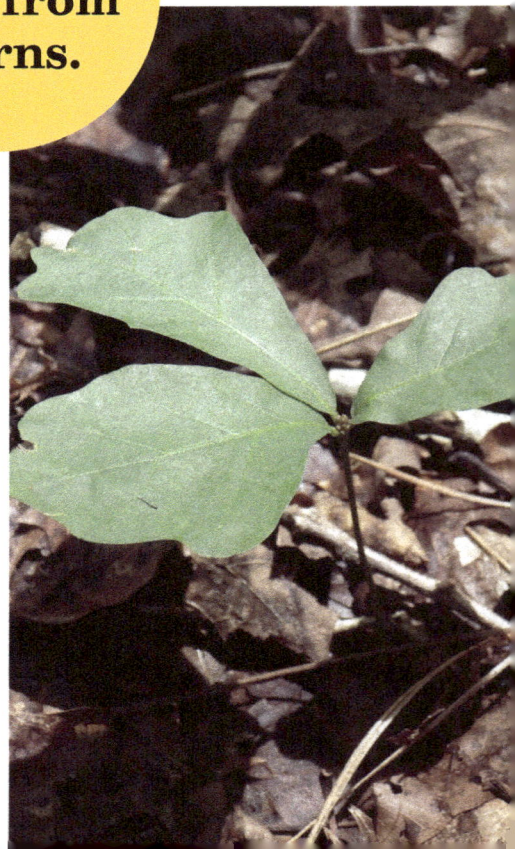

My nose says a squirrel ran up that oak tree.

I see it. It's eating an acorn. Squirrels love acorns. Acorns are nuts from oak trees. Bears, deer, and turkeys love acorns, too.

Bang, bang, bang. That's the sound falling acorns make when they hit and bounce off my roof.

Oak trees are important to people and wildlife. They provide food, warmth, and shelter.

For these reasons, the oak is the national tree of the United States.

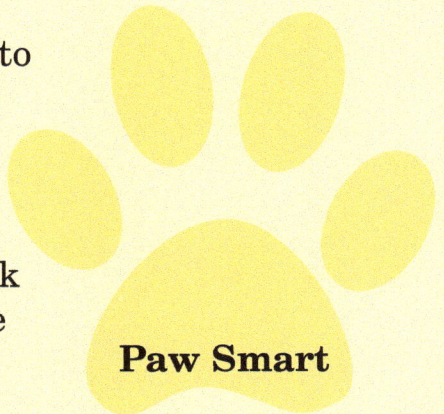

Paw Smart

Bark helps trees breathe.

Be like me and touch a tree.

You're touching bark. Tree bark is the outside part of trees and bushes. It might have scars, bumps, colorful stripes, or sharp thorns.

How does it feel? My old oak tree feels rough because it has tree wrinkles. My apple tree feels smoother.

Bark protects trees from insects, animals, fire, sun, and wind.

As some trees get older and bigger, their bark gets thicker and cracks. Cracks make bark feel rougher.

Paw Smart

Anoles are fast climbers.

That green anole jumped and ran up the tree!

Anoles are lizards. They tilt and bob their heads, do push-ups, and sunbathe. Males puff out their throats to say "Hi!" to females.

Like hawks, anoles are hunters. Sometimes I see one eating a spider, cricket, or worm.

As you get bigger, your skin grows.

Lizards and snakes shed their skins to get bigger ones. They don't grow skin like people and dogs do.

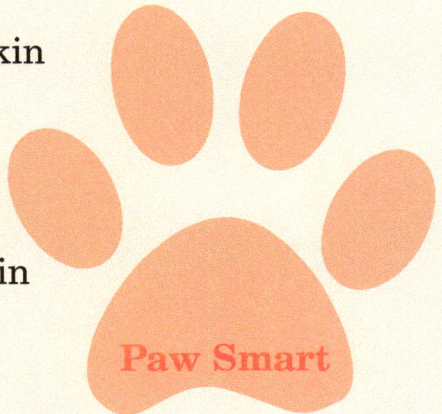

Paw Smart

Box turtles live on land.

See that moving painted rock?

It's a box turtle. It will eat almost anything. Turtles think worms, slugs, spiders, berries, and even dead snakes are delicious.

Don't touch, Phoebe! Touching scares them. A scared turtle pulls its head, legs, and tail into its shell. The shell closes like a box for protection.

How can you tell if a box turtle is male or female? Look at its eyes.

Most males have red eyes. Females usually have golden brown eyes.

Paw Smart

Mushrooms
grow
super fast.

Hey, that turtle's eating a mushroom!

After a good rain, my yard gets mushrooms in many shapes, sizes, and colors. Some grow alone. Others grow in groups.

Look at one. Do you see an egg, umbrella, or flower? Is it smaller than a paw or wider than your head?

People and dogs should only touch and eat mushrooms from the store.

Box turtles and squirrels can eat mushrooms found outside, but not us. Wild mushrooms can make us sick.

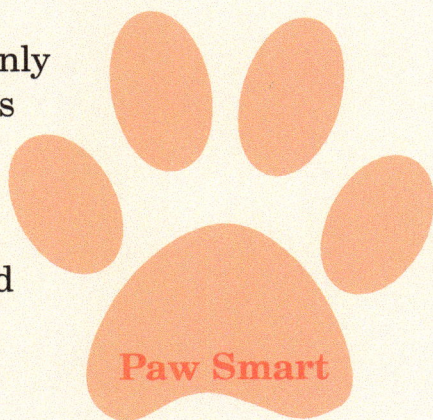

Paw Smart

Bees have five eyes.

Ever watch bees fly?

Let's visit my garden. Bees go there for food found in flowers. Hear buzzing? Bees and other insects buzz when they flap their wings very fast.

Sometimes a bee lands on me. Silly bee! I am not a flower. If I stand still, it will fly away.

Solitary bees live alone. Social bees live together in hives.

Honeybees are social bees. They make honey from sugary juice called nectar. Bees get nectar from flowers.

Paw Smart

Chickens
recognize
people.

Chickens are funny. Ever meet one?

Six chickens live at that house. Watch them kick leaves, scratch the ground, and jump for insects. They get excited when fed corn, grapes, or cooked spaghetti noodles.

Exploring can lead to new friends. Making friends means we had a great day!

Female birds are hens. They lay eggs. Egg size and color differs by bird.

Chicken hens often sing when laying eggs. Their eggs are brown, cream, white, blue, or green.

Paw Smart

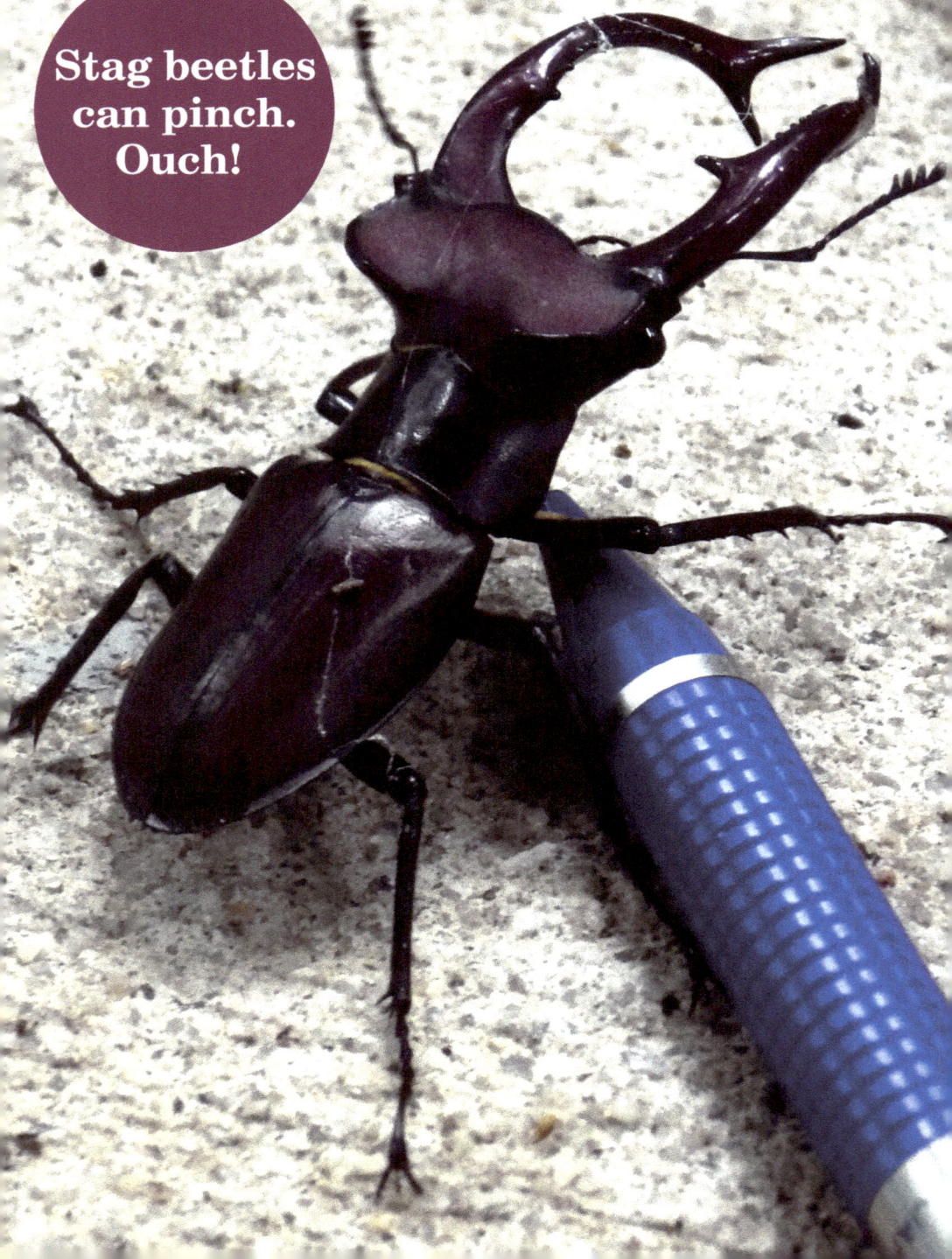

Stag beetles
can pinch.
Ouch!

What is *that* walking on my front porch?

Look at the huge jaw. It looks like it has crab claws. Imagine us with jaws like that!

Asking around, we're told it is a stag beetle. Its babies help keep forests healthy. They turn dead trees into food for other plants.

Stag is another name for deer. The stag beetle was named by people who thought its jaws were antlers.

This beetle is also called a pinching bug. Don't pick one up!

Paw Smart

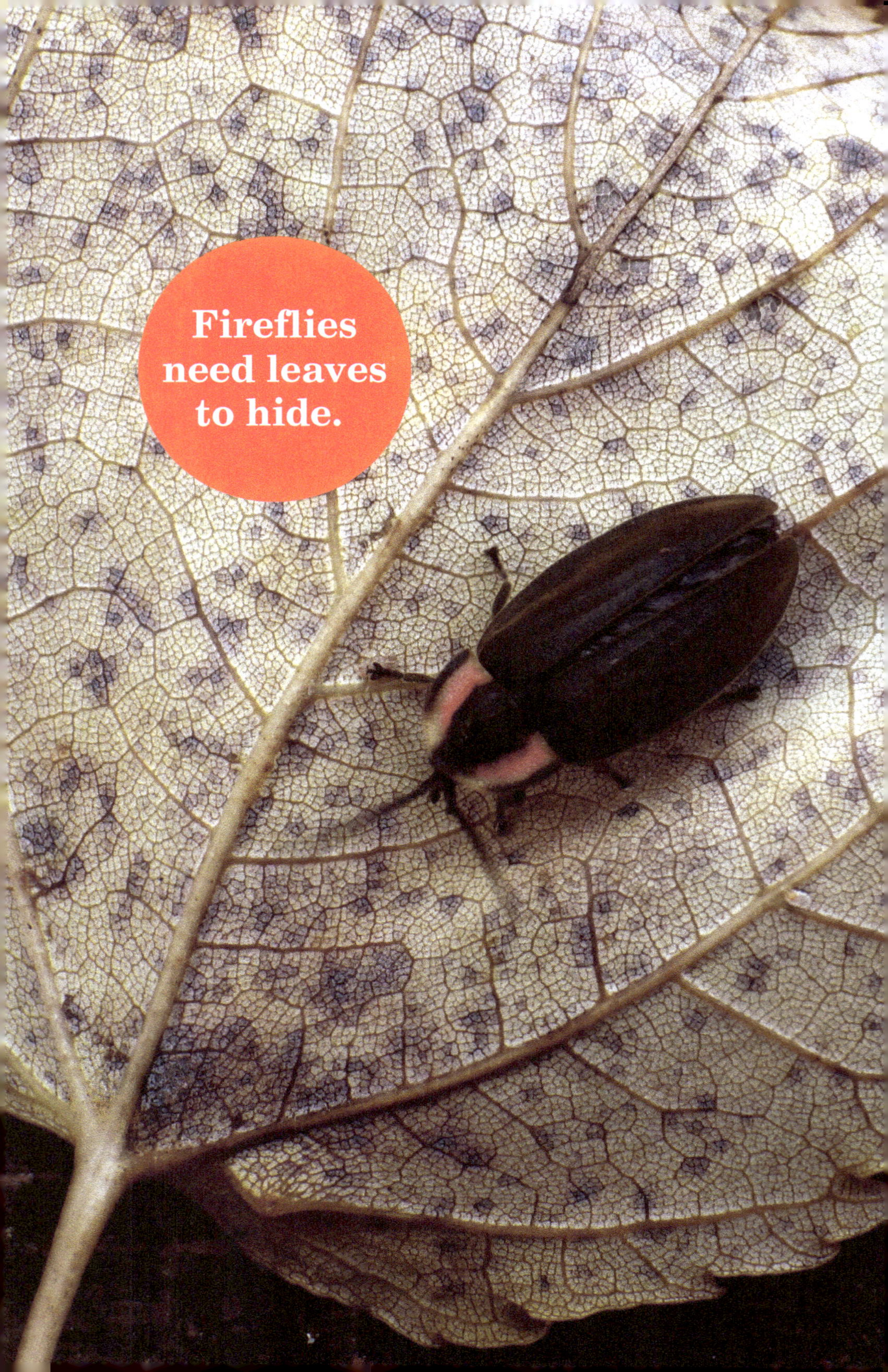

Fireflies need leaves to hide.

It's getting dark. It's summer, so look for tiny flying lights.

Fireflies make those lights. Instead of using voices, they speak by turning lights on and off like a lamp. They need darkness to talk.

Some fireflies can't make light. They talk during the day by making smells called pheromones.

Nicknamed lightning bugs, fireflies are beetles. Beetles, flies, ants, and bees are insects. Insects have six legs.

Spiders have eight legs. Worms don't have legs. Are they insects?

Paw Smart

Frogs sleep with their eyes open.

As we watch for fireflies,
listen to those frogs.

Bullfrogs rumble. Spring
peepers chirp. Green tree
frogs say "queenk." Pickerel
frogs seem to snore. That
splash means a frog went
swimming.

Frogs are noisy especially at
night and on rainy days. If
their noise stops, an animal
may be near.

Frogs do not need
flashlights. Scientists think
frogs may see better at
night than any other
animal.

In the dark, frogs see colors
where we only see black.

Paw Smart

Tadpoles live in water like fish.

See the frog eggs in my pond?

Each egg contains a tadpole. When eggs hatch, the tadpoles look like fish with fat heads and long tails.

I like watching tadpoles turn into frogs. They grow legs and lose their tail. Unlike us, frogs mostly drink and breathe through their skin.

Most frogs lay jelly-covered eggs in water. The jelly soaks up water to protect the eggs.

Some frogs lay eggs in clumps. Toad eggs are put inside jelly-like rope.

Paw Smart

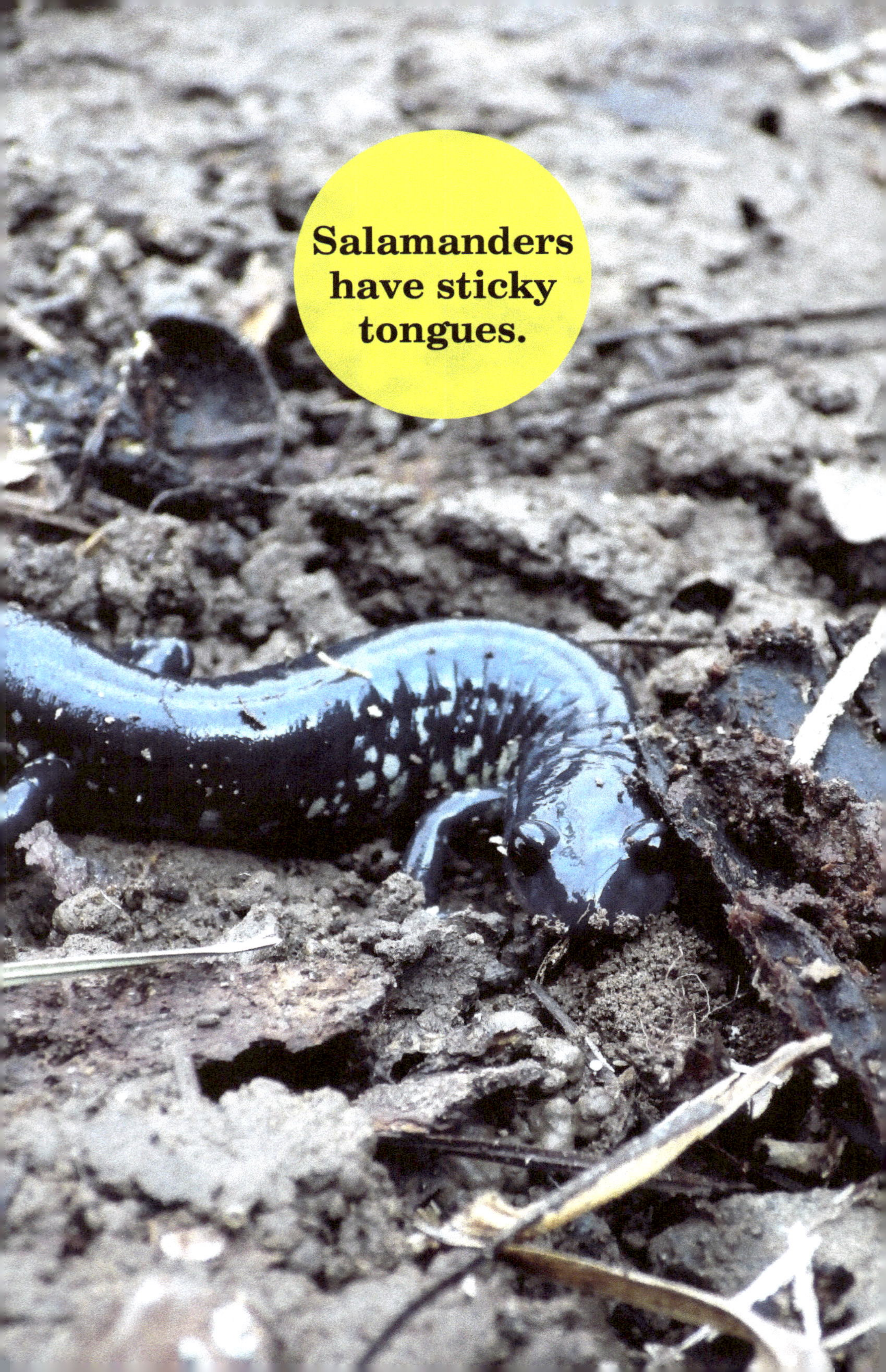

Salamanders have sticky tongues.

I think salamanders are cute. What about you?

I once found one under a log and another under a rock. Salamanders live in the woods and sleep in dark damp places.

Many salamanders become slimy when scared. Their slime tastes bad and is hard to remove from fingers and paws.

Salamanders look like lizards, but have smooth, wet skin like many frogs.

Most salamanders are nocturnal. Nocturnal animals sleep during the day and look for food at night.

Paw Smart

What is behind that door?

Our neighbors say they have a fairy door. Let's find it.

There it is, at the bottom of the tree. When we open it, we can enter a magical world.

The neighborhood children say they see and talk to fairies. Let's use our imagination. What will we see and do?

Look. Listen. Sniff. That's the Odie way to explore. Phoebe and I are always finding interesting surprises.

Try it. Walk with a friend. What will you find?

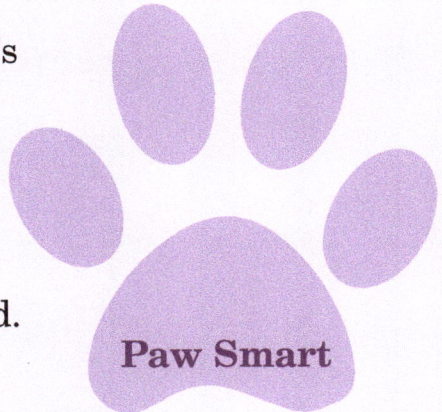

Paw Smart

Glossary

Antler: a horn on top of a deer's head

Bob: move a head quickly up and down

Chirp: a fast, cheerful noise

Cream: a color that is almost white or very light brown

Explore: to learn something new

Explorer: someone who likes to learn

Fairies: super nice, magical creatures that fly

Flapping: moving a wing or arm up and down

Fuzzy: very soft, short, curly material

Hatch: when a baby bird comes out of an egg

Hives: where social bees live

Imagination: making up stories

Magical: making fun, surprising things happen

Neighbor: a person who lives near you

Neighborhood: where you and your neighbors live

Odie (O-d):   the nickname of Odin, a happy dog with his own books

Pest: unwanted insect or small animal that harms or destroys plants

Glossary

Puff: making something larger with air

Rough: very bumpy to the touch

Rumble: a noise that sounds heavy and slow

Shed: skin or hair falling off so new skin or hair can grow

Shelter: housing or other cover that keeps one safe and dry in bad weather or danger

Slimy: feeling slippery and sticky

Smooth: flat to the touch; not bumpy

Speckled: having many spots of different sizes

Wild: a plant or animal living outside without help from people

Phoebe loves splashing.

Acknowledgments

My husband for his editing prowess and recognizing our need for another family member

My parents for their love of dogs and books

Amy Stawarz for her amazing, award-winning graphic design skills

Daniel Dombrowski, D.V.M., of the North Carolina Museum of Natural Sciences (Raleigh, NC) for his wide-ranging animal expertise

Janice Monaco for her publication expertise

Friends for their book development insight and support:
    Richard Adamski
    Lesley, Brian, Hannah & Gretchen Bradley
    Linda Cale
    Anne Getzenberg
    Margaret Griffin
    Susan Groh
    Amy, John, Tommy, Colin & Ryan Marshall
    Cara, Nate, Mckinley, Dallin & Afton Nicholes
    Julie Tapp
    Nikole, Adam, Roni & Nava Van Goor
    Grace Li Wang

Special Thanks

The Society for the Prevention of Cruelty to Animals (SPCA) of Wake County (North Carolina) rescued Odie from the streets when he was three months old. The staff and volunteers gave him love, taught him manners, and found him a good forever home. Odie enjoys daily walks, tummy rubs, and doggy cookies.

Odie is a happy dog.

If you are considering adopting a new friend and sharing fun adventures, please visit a rescue organization such as your local SPCA, other humane organizations, or county animal shelter. For suggestions, these websites can help:

www.guidestar.org/NonprofitDirectory.aspx
www.petfinder.com
dog.rescueshelter.com
www.animalshelter.org

Thanks for reading!

Odie's first book is titled *Meet Odie*. In it, he tells you about himself: why he reads with his nose, wears a dog tag, loves walks, and other fun facts. It is available from local bookstores and Amazon.

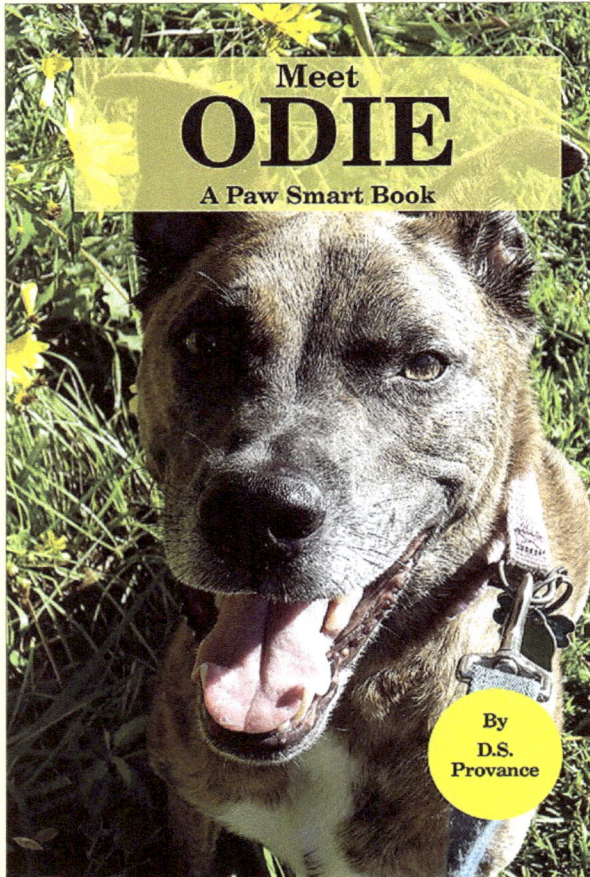

Meet
ODIE
A Paw Smart Book

By
D.S.
Provance

www.ingramcontent.com/pod-product-compliance
Lightning Source LLC
Chambersburg PA
CBHW042249040426
42336CB00044B/3389